Baby
Washcloths &
Afghan Squares™

Lisa Carnahan

Annie's®

Introduction

Looking for a simple yet beautiful gift for that new one? Look no further than this baby blocks collection. This book includes instructions for 10 easy-to-knit blocks, each featuring a different textured pattern. Also included are instructions for a block with a slip-stitch pattern; this block is worked 10 times, with each block using different colors for the stripes.

Worked in a soft cotton yarn and sewn together, the 20 blocks create a lovely baby blanket. Knit individually, they work equally well as washcloths for bath time.

The textured patterns are very geometric—diamonds, squares, basket weaves, circles, zigzag and more. I'm sure you'll enjoy the variety of stitch patterns as you work each 8-inch block. Special consideration was taken that the blocks do not have any lace holes or strands of yarn to catch little fingers or toes.

So grab your yarn and needles and get started on this fun, portable and always interesting project!

Meet the Designer

My mother taught me to knit when I was 9 or 10 years old, but it wasn't until I was in my 20s that I picked up the needles again, and I haven't put them down since. What started out as a hobby, knitting for my three children, has become a full-time career. I began knitting model garments for the yarn industry, and at the same time working on some of my own designs.

I then began doing freelance designing, and my patterns have appeared in the collections of Classic Elite, Fiber Trends, Tahki Stacy Charles, Lion Brand Yarns and others. They have been published by Annie's and Interweave Press. In 2001, I launched my own business, Lisa Knits, a line of knitwear patterns that are available in yarn shops across the country.

Table of Contents

....

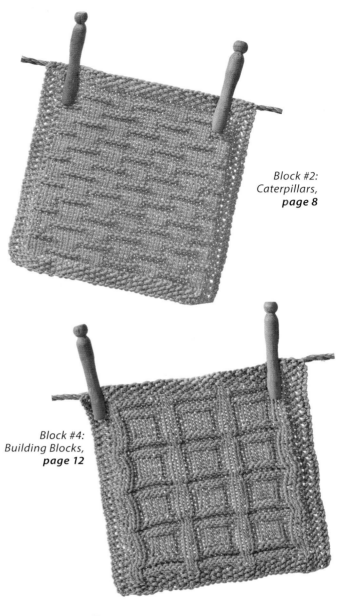

*Block #2:
Caterpillars,
page 8*

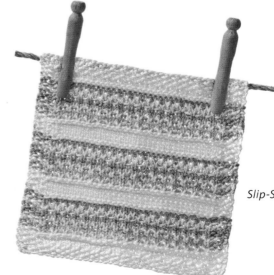

*Block #4:
Building Blocks,
page 12*

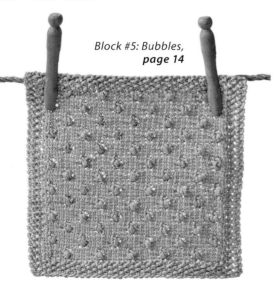

*Block #5: Bubbles,
page 14*

*Block #11:
Slip-Stitch Block,
page 26*

Basic Block &
Afghan Information

Finished Measurements
Block: 8 x 8 inches
Afghan: 32 x 40 inches

Materials
- Tahki Yarns Cotton Classic (DK
  weight; 100% mercerized cotton;
  108 yds/50g per hank): 6 hanks
  butter yellow #3548 (A); 2 hanks each coral
  #3473 (B), leaf green #3716 (C),
  soft turquoise #3816 (D), light denim #3847 (E)
  and light wisteria #3915 (F)
- Size 7 (4.5mm) needles or size needed to
  obtain gauge
- Stitch markers (optional)

3 LIGHT

Gauge
20 sts and 28 rows = 4 inches/10cm in St st.

To save time, take time to check gauge.

Pattern Notes
The afghan consists of 20 blocks: 1 each of the
10 different-color textured blocks and 10 slip-stitch
blocks that are worked with 1 main color and
2 contrasting colors that vary with each block.

Each textured block requires approximately 70 yards.
Each slip-stitch block requires approximately
50 yards of A (main color) and 14 yards each of
2 contrasting colors.

Each block begins and ends with 41 stitches.
The borders are worked in Seed stitch and the
centers are worked in the different pattern stitches.
If desired, place markers between the 4-stitch
Seed stitch borders and the main pattern stitches.
See each block for the pattern stitches.

Finishing
With A and using whipstitch or mattress stitch seam,
sew blocks together create a 4-column, 5-row check-
erboard of textured blocks (Blocks 1–10) and slip-
stitch blocks (Blocks 11A–11J) in any order desired. ●

Skill Level
 EASY

Finished Measurements
Block: 8 x 8 inches

Materials
- Tahki Yarns Cotton Classic (DK weight; 100% mercerized cotton; 108 yds/ 50g per hank): 1 hank soft turquoise #3816 (D)
- Size 7 (4.5mm) needles or size needed to obtain gauge
- Stitch markers (optional)

Pattern Stitches
Seed st (odd number of sts)
Row 1: K1, *p1, k1; rep from * to end.
Rep Row 1 for pat.

Block #1 (multiple of 12 sts + 9)
Row 1 (RS): *K9, p1, k1, p1; rep from * once, k9.
Row 2: K1, p7, *[k1, p1] twice, k1, p7; rep from * once, k1.
Row 3: *K1, p1, k5, [p1, k1] twice, p1; rep from * once, k1, p1, k5, p1, k1.
Row 4: K1, p1, k1, *p3, k1, p1, k1; rep from * to end.
Row 5: *[K1, p1] 4 times, k4; rep from * once, [k1, p1] 4 times, k1.

Row 6: P2, [k1, p1] twice, k1, *p7, [k1, p1] twice, k1; rep from * once, p2.
Row 7: *K3, p1, k1, p1, k6; rep from * once, k3, p1, k1, p1, k3.
Row 8: Rep Row 6.
Row 9: Rep Row 5.
Row 10: Rep Row 4.
Row 11: Rep Row 3.
Row 12: Rep Row 2.
Rep Rows 1–12 for pat.

Block
With D, cast on 41 sts.

Work 5 rows in Seed st.

Set-up row (RS): Work 4 sts in Seed st, work Row 1 of Block #1 pat, work 4 sts in established Seed st.

Maintaining 4 sts in Seed st at each side, complete 4 reps of 12-row Block #1 pat, then work Rows 1–6.

Work 4 rows in Seed st.

Bind off all sts in pat.

Finishing
Weave in all ends.

Block to 8 inches square. ●

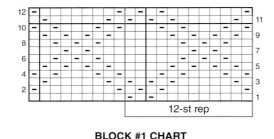

STITCH KEY
☐ K on RS, p on WS
⊟ P on RS, k on WS

BLOCK #1 CHART

Baby Washcloths & Afghan Squares

Block #2: Caterpillars

Skill Level
■■□□ EASY

Finished Measurements
Block: 8 x 8 inches

Materials
- Tahki Yarns Cotton Classic (DK weight; 100% mercerized cotton; 108 yds/ 50g per hank): 1 hank coral #3473 (B)
- Size 7 (4.5mm) needles or size needed to obtain gauge
- Stitch markers (optional)

Special Abbreviation
Make 1 Purlwise (M1-P): Insert LH needle from front to back under horizontal strand between last st worked and next st on LH needle; purl through back of resulting loop.

Pattern Stitches
Seed st (odd number of sts)
Row 1: K1, *p1, k1; rep from * to end.
Rep Row 1 for pat.

Block #2 (multiple of 10 sts + 2)
Row 1 (RS): K32.

Row 2 and all WS rows: P32.
Row 3: [K3, p6, k1] 3 times, k2.
Row 5: K32.
Row 7: [P4, k4, p2] 3 times, p2.
Row 8: P32.
Rep Rows 1–8 for pat.

Block
With B, cast on 41 sts.

Work 5 rows in Seed st.

Set-up row (RS): Work 4 sts in Seed st, work Row 1 of Block #2 pat and dec 1 st using k2tog, work 4 sts in established Seed st—40 sts.

Maintaining 4 sts in Seed st at each side, complete 6 reps of 8-row Block #2 pat, then work Rows 1–5.

Inc row (WS): Work 4 sts in Seed st, p32, M1-P, work 4 sts in Seed st—41 sts.

Work 4 rows in Seed st.

Bind off all sts in pat.

Finishing
Weave in all ends.

Block to 8 inches square. •

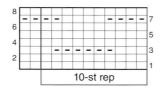

BLOCK #2 CHART

STITCH KEY
☐ K on RS, p on WS
⊟ P on RS

Block #3: Gum Balls

Skill Level

◖■■□□ EASY

Finished Measurements
Block: 8 x 8 inches

Materials
- Tahki Yarns Cotton Classic (DK weight; 100% mercerized cotton; 108 yds/ 50g per hank): 1 hank light wisteria #3915 (F)
- Size 7 (4.5mm) needles or size needed to obtain gauge
- Stitch markers (optional)

Pattern Stitches
Seed st (odd number of sts)
Row 1: K1, *p1, k1; rep from * to end.
Rep Row 1 for pat.

Block #3 (multiple of 10 sts + 3)
Rows 1 and 3 (RS): K33.
Rows 2 and 4: P33.
Row 5: [K3, p2, k5] 3 times, k3.
Row 6: P3, [p4, k4, p2] 3 times.
Rows 7 and 9: [K1, p6, k3] 3 times, k3.
Row 8: P3, [p3, k6, p1] 3 times.
Row 10: Rep Row 6.
Row 11: Rep Row 5.

Rows 12, 14 and 16: P33.
Rows 13 and 15: K33.
Row 17: K3, [k5, p2, k3] 3 times.
Row 18: [P2, k4, p4] 3 times, p3.
Rows 19 and 21: K3, [k3, p6, k1] 3 times.
Row 20: [P1, k6, p3] 3 times, p3.
Row 22: Rep Row 18.
Row 23: Rep Row 17.
Row 24: P33.
Rep Rows 1–24 for pat.

Block
With F, cast on 41 sts.

Work 5 rows in Seed st.

Set-up row (RS): Work 4 sts in Seed st, work Row 1 of Block #3 pat across next 33 sts, work 4 sts in established Seed st.

Maintaining 4 sts in Seed st each side, complete 2 reps of 24-row Block #3 pat, then work Rows 1–4.

Work 4 rows in Seed st.

Bind off all sts in pat.

Finishing
Weave in all ends.

Block to 8 inches square. ●

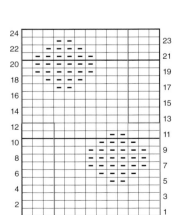

BLOCK #3 CHART

STITCH KEY
□ K on RS, p on WS
⊟ P on RS, k on WS

Block #4: Building Blocks

Skill Level
◼◼◻◻ EASY

Finished Measurements
Block: 8 x 8 inches

Materials
- Tahki Yarns Cotton Classic (DK weight; 100% mercerized cotton; 108 yds/ 50g per hank): 1 hank leaf green #3716 (C)
- Size 7 (4.5mm) needles or size needed to obtain gauge
- Stitch markers (optional)

Special Abbreviation
Make 1 (M1): Insert LH needle from front to back under horizontal strand between last st worked and next st on LH needle; knit through back of resulting loop.

Pattern Stitches
Seed st (odd number of sts)
Row 1: K1, *p1, k1; rep from * to end.
Rep Row 1 for pat.

Block #4 (multiple of 10 sts + 2)
Row 1 (RS): K32.
Row 2: P32.
Row 3: [K2, p8] 3 times, k2.

Row 4: P2, [k8, p2] 3 times.
Rows 5, 7 and 9: [K2, p2, k4, p2] 3 times, k2.
Rows 6, 8 and 10: P2, [k2, p4, k2, p2] 3 times.
Row 11: Rep Row 3.
Row 12: Rep Row 4.
Rep Rows 1–12 for pat.

Block
With C, cast on 41 sts.

Work 5 rows in Seed st.

Set-up row (RS): Work 4 sts in Seed st, k2tog, k1, [p8, k2] 3 times, work 4 sts in established Seed st—40 sts.

Next row: Work 4 sts in Seed st, p2, [k8, p2] 3 times, work 4 sts in established Seed st.

Maintaining 4 sts in Seed st at each side, work 12-row Block #4 pat 4 times, then work Rows 1–3.

Inc row (WS): Work 4 sts in Seed st, work Row 4 of Block #4 pat, M1, work 4 sts in Seed st—41 sts.

Work 4 rows in Seed st.

Bind off all sts in pat.

Finishing
Weave in all ends.

Block to 8 inches square. ●

BLOCK #4 CHART

10-st rep

STITCH KEY
☐ K on RS, p on WS
⊟ P on RS, k on WS

Block #5: Bubbles

Skill Level
■■□□ EASY

Finished Measurements
Block: 8 x 8 inches

Materials
- Tahki Yarns Cotton Classic (DK weight; 100% mercerized cotton; 108 yds/ 50g per hank): 1 hank light denim #3847 (E)
- Size 7 (4.5mm) needles or size needed to obtain gauge
- Stitch markers (optional)

Special Abbreviation
Knot St: Knit into the front loop, back loop, front loop and back loop of same st; pass first 3 sts over last st.

Pattern Stitches
Seed st (odd number of sts)
Row 1: K1, *p1, k1; rep from * to end.
Rep Row 1 for pat.

Block #5 (multiple of 6 sts + 3)
Row 1 (RS): K33.
Row 2 and all WS rows: P33.
Row 3: [K4, Knot St, k1] 5 times, k3.
Row 5: K33.
Row 7: [K1, Knot St, k4] 5 times, k1, Knot St, k1.
Row 8: P33.
Rep Rows 1–8 for pat.

Block
With E, cast on 41 sts.

Work 5 rows in Seed st.

Set-up row (RS): Work 4 sts in Seed st, work Row 1 of Block #5 pat across 33 sts, work 4 sts in established Seed st.

Maintaining 4 sts in Seed st each side, complete 6 reps of 8-row Block #5 pat, then work Rows 1–4.

Work 4 rows in Seed st.

Bind off all sts in pat.

Finishing
Weave in all ends.

Block to 8 inches square. ●

BLOCK #5 CHART

STITCH KEY
□ K on RS, p on WS
Ⓓ Knot St

Block #6: A-Tisket, A-Tasket

Skill Level
◼◻◻◻ EASY

Finished Measurements
Block: 8 x 8 inches

Materials
- Tahki Yarns Cotton Classic (DK weight; 100% mercerized cotton; 108 yds/ 50g per hank): 1 hank soft turquoise #3816 (D)
- Size 7 (4.5mm) needles or size needed to obtain gauge
- Stitch markers (optional)

Special Abbreviation
Make 1 (M1): Insert LH needle from front to back under horizontal strand between last st worked and next st on LH needle; knit through back of resulting loop.

Pattern Stitches
Seed st (odd number of sts)
Row 1: K1, *p1, k1; rep from * to end.
Rep Row 1 for pat.

Block #6 (multiple of 8 sts + 3)
Row 1 and all RS rows: [K3, p1] 8 times, k3.

Rows 2, 4 and 6: P3, [k5, p3] 4 times.
Rows 8, 10 and 12: K3, [k1, p3, k4] 4 times.
Rep Rows 1–12 for pat.

Block
With D, cast on 41 sts.

Work 5 rows in Seed st.

Set-up row (RS): Work 4 sts in Seed st, M1, k2, p1, [k3, p1] 7 times, k2, M1, work 4 sts in established Seed st—43 sts. *Note: This counts as Row 1 of first pat rep.*

Maintaining 4 sts in Seed st at each side, beg with Row 2 of Block #6 pat, complete 4 reps of 12-row pat, then work Rows 1–5.

Dec row (WS): Work 4 sts in Seed st, p2tog, p1, [k5, p3] 3 times, k5, p1, p2tog, work 4 sts in Seed st—41 sts.

Work 4 rows in Seed st.

Bind off all sts in pat.

Finishing
Weave in all ends.

Block to 8 inches square. ●

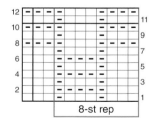

BLOCK #6 CHART

STITCH KEY
☐ K on RS, p on WS
⊟ P on RS, k on WS

Block #7: Zigzag

Skill Level
■ ■ □ □ EASY

Finished Measurements
Block: 8 x 8 inches

Materials
- Tahki Yarns Cotton Classic (DK weight; 100% mercerized cotton; 108 yds/ 50g per hank): 1 hank coral #3473 (B)
- Size 7 (4.5mm) needles or size needed to obtain gauge
- Stitch markers (optional)

Pattern Stitches
Seed st (odd number of sts)
Row 1: K1, *p1, k1; rep from * to end.
Rep Row 1 for pat.

Block #7 (multiple of 8 sts + 1)
Row 1 (RS): [K1, p7] 4 times, k1.
Row 2 and all WS rows: Work the sts as they present themselves (knit the knit sts and purl the purl sts).
Row 3: [K2, p5, k1] 4 times, k1.
Row 5: [K3, p3, k2] 4 times, k1.
Row 7: [K4, p1, k3] 4 times, k1.

Row 9: [P1, k7] 4 times, p1.
Row 11: [P2, k5, p1] 4 times, p1.
Row 13: [P3, k3, p2] 4 times, p1.
Row 15: [P4, k1, p3] 4 times, p1.
Row 16: Rep Row 2.
Rep Rows 1–16 for pat.

Block
With B, cast on 41 sts.

Work 5 rows in Seed st.

Set-up row 1 (RS): Work 4 sts in Seed st, purl to last 4 sts, work 4 sts in established Seed st—40 sts.

Set-up row 2: Work 4 sts in Seed st, knit to last 4 sts, work 4 sts in established Seed st—40 sts.

Maintaining 4 sts in Seed st at each side, work 3 reps of 16-row Block #7 pat.

Rep Set-up rows 1 and 2.

Work 4 rows in Seed st.

Bind off all sts in pat.

Finishing
Weave in all ends.

Block to 8 inches square. ●

BLOCK #7 CHART

STITCH KEY
□ K on RS, p on WS
⊟ P on RS, k on WS

8-st rep

Block #8: Triangles

Skill Level
 EASY

Finished Measurements
Block: 8 x 8 inches

Materials
- Tahki Yarns Cotton Classic (DK weight; 100% mercerized cotton; 108 yds/50g per hank): 1 hank light wisteria #3915 (F)
- Size 7 (4.5mm) needles or size needed to obtain gauge
- Stitch markers (optional)

Special Abbreviation
Make 1 Purlwise (M1-P): Insert LH needle from front to back under horizontal strand between last st worked and next st on LH needle; purl through back of resulting loop.

Pattern Stitches
Seed st (odd number of sts)
Row 1: K1, *p1, k1; rep from * to end.
Rep Row 1 for pat.

Block #8 (multiple of 5 sts + 1)
Row 1 (RS): [K4, p1] 8 times, k1.
Row 2 and all WS rows: P31.

Row 3: [K3, p2] 8 times, k1.
Row 5: [K2, p3] 8 times, k1.
Row 7: [K1, p4] 8 times, k1.
Row 9: P31.
Row 10: P31.
Rep Rows 1–10 for pat.

Block
With F, cast on 41 sts.

Work 5 rows in Seed st.

Set-up row 1 (RS): Work 4 sts in Seed st, k2tog, knit to last 6 sts, ssk, work 4 sts in established Seed st—39 sts.

Set-up row 2: Work 4 sts in Seed st, purl to last 4 sts, work 4 sts in established Seed st.

Maintaining 4 sts in Seed st at each side, work 4 reps of 10-row Block #8 pat, then work Rows 1–9.

Inc row (WS): Work 4 sts in Seed st, M1-P, purl to last 4 sts, M1-P, work 4 sts in Seed st—41 sts.

Work 4 rows in Seed st.

Bind off all sts in pat.

Finishing
Weave in all ends.

Block to 8 inches square. ●

5-st rep

BLOCK #8 CHART

STITCH KEY
☐ K on RS, p on WS
⊟ P on RS, k on WS

Block #9: Bugs

Skill Level
■■□□ EASY

Finished Measurements
Block: 8 x 8 inches

Materials
- Tahki Yarns Cotton Classic (DK weight; 100% mercerized cotton; 108 yds/ 50g per hank): 1 hank leaf green #3716 (C)
- Size 7 (4.5mm) needles or size needed to obtain gauge
- Stitch markers (optional)

Special Abbreviations
Knit in row below (K1B): Insert RH needle into center of st 1 row below next st on LH needle; k1, dropping st from LH needle.

Make 1 Purlwise (M1-P): Insert LH needle from front to back under horizontal strand between last st worked and next st on LH needle; purl through back of resulting loop.

Pattern Stitches
Seed st (odd number of sts)
Row 1: K1, *p1, k1; rep from * to end.
Rep Row 1 for pat.

Block #9 (multiple of 6 sts + 2)
Row 1 (RS): K32.
Row 2: P1, [p3, k3] 5 times, p1.
Row 3: K1, [p1, K1B, p1, k3] 5 times, k1.
Row 4: P32.
Row 5: K32.
Row 6: P1, [k3, p3] 5 times, p1.
Row 7: K1, [k3, p1, K1B, p1] 5 times, k1.
Row 8: P32.
Rep Rows 1–8 for pat.

Block
With C, cast on 41 sts.

Work 5 rows in Seed st.

Set-up row (RS): Work 4 sts in Seed st, k2tog, k31, work 4 sts in established Seed st—40 sts.
Note: This counts as Row 1 on first rep of Block #9 pat.

Maintaining 4 sts in Seed st at each side and beg with Row 2, complete 6 reps of 8-row Block #9 pat, then work Rows 1–3.

Inc row (WS): Work 4 sts in Seed st, purl to last 4 sts, M1-P, work 4 sts in Seed st—41 sts.

Work 4 rows in Seed st.

Bind off all sts in pat.

Finishing
Weave in all ends.

Block to 8 inches square. ●

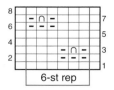

BLOCK #9 CHART

STITCH KEY	
□	K on RS, p on WS
–	P on RS, k on WS
∩	K1B

Block #10: 3-D Blocks

Skill Level
■■□□ EASY

Finished Measurements
Block: 8 x 8 inches

Materials
- Tahki Yarns Cotton Classic (DK weight; 100% mercerized cotton; 108 yds/ 50g per hank): 1 hank light denim #3847 (E)
- Size 7 (4.5mm) needles or size needed to obtain gauge
- Stitch markers (optional)

3 LIGHT

Special Abbreviation
Make 1 (M1): Insert LH needle from front to back under horizontal strand between last st worked and next st on LH needle; knit through back of resulting loop.

Pattern Stitches
Seed st (odd number of sts)
Row 1: K1, *p1, k1; rep from * to end.
Rep Row 1 for pat.

Block #10 (multiple of 10 sts + 2)
Row 1 (RS): [K1, p1] 16 times.
Row 2: K1, *p2, [k1, p1] 3 times, k2; rep from * twice, p1.
Row 3: K1, *p3, [k1, p1] twice, k3; rep from * twice, p1.
Row 4: K1, *p4, k1, p1, k4; rep from * twice, p1.
Rows 5 and 6: K1, *p5, k5; rep from * twice, p1.
Row 7: P1, *k1, p4, k4, p1; rep from * twice, k1.
Row 8: K1, *p1, k1, p3, k3, p1, k1; rep from * twice, p1.
Row 9: P1, *k1, p1, k1, p2, k2, p1, k1, p1; rep from * twice, k1.
Row 10: [K1, p1] 16 times.
Row 11: [P1, k1] 16 times.
Row 12: K1, *p1, k1, p1, k2, p2, k1, p1, k1; rep from * twice, p1.
Row 13: P1, *k1, p1, k3, p3, k1, p1; rep from * twice, k1.
Row 14: K1, *p1, k4, p4, k1; rep from * twice, p1.
Rows 15 and 16: P1, *k5, p5; rep from * twice, k1.

Row 17: P1, *k4, p1, k1, p4; rep from * twice, k1.
Row 18: P1, *k3, [p1, k1] twice, p3; rep from * twice, k1.
Row 19: P1, *k2, [p1, k1] 3 times, p2; rep from * twice, k1.
Row 20: [P1, k1] 16 times.
Rep Rows 1–20 for pat.

Block
With E, cast on 41 sts.

Work 5 rows in Seed st.

Set-up row (RS): Work 4 sts in Seed st, [k1, p1] 15 times, k1, p2tog, work 4 sts in established Seed st—40 sts.

Maintaining 4 sts in Seed st at each side and beg with Row 2, complete 2 reps of 20-row Block #10 pat, then work Rows 1–11.

Inc row (WS): Work 4 sts in Seed st, work Row 12 of Block #10 pat, M1, work 4 sts in Seed st—41 sts.

Work 4 rows in Seed st.

Bind off all sts in pat.

Finishing
Weave in all ends.

Block to 8 inches square. ●

STITCH KEY
☐ K on RS, p on WS
– P on RS, k on WS

10-st rep

BLOCK #10 CHART

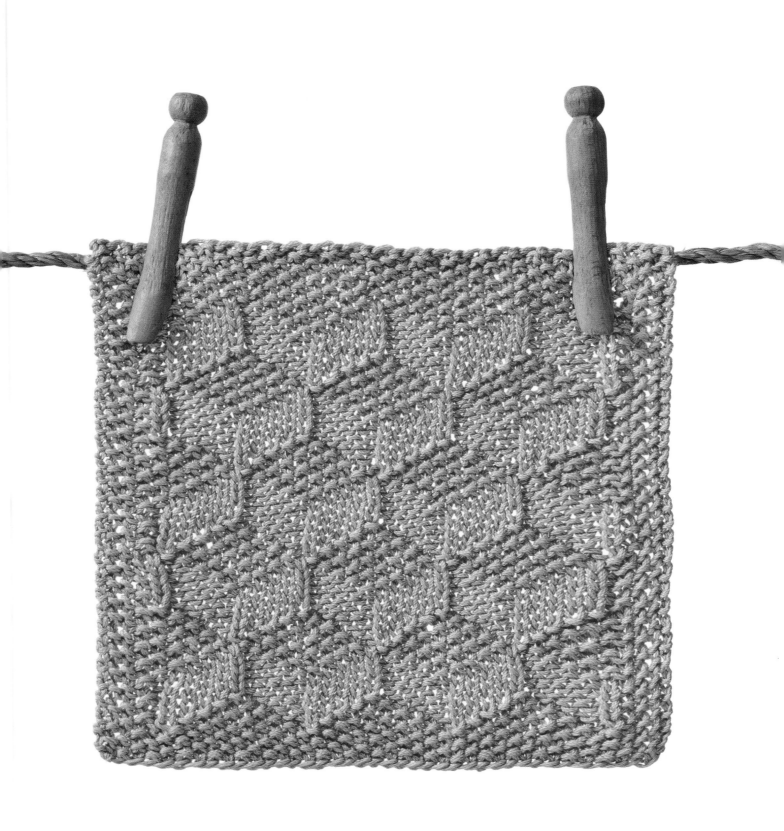

Skill Level
■■□□ EASY

Finished Measurements
Block: 8 x 8 inches

Materials
- Tahki Yarns Cotton Classic (DK weight; 100% mercerized cotton; 108 yds/ 50g per hank): 1 hank butter yellow #3548 (A); 1 hank each coral #3473 (B), leaf green #3716 (C), soft turquoise #3816 (D), light denim #3847 (E) and light wisteria #3915 (F)
- Size 7 (4.5mm) needles or size needed to obtain gauge
- Stitch markers (optional)

Make 10 blocks, using butter yellow (A) as MC for all, and contrasting colors as follows:

11A: CC1 = D, CC2 = B

11B: CC1 = F, CC2 = C

11C: CC1 = E, CC2 = D

11D: CC1 = B, CC2 = F

11E: CC1 = C, CC2 = E

11F: CC1 = D, CC2 = F

11G: CC1 = B, CC2 = C

11H: CC1 = F, CC2 = E

11I: CC1 = C, CC2 = D

11J: CC1 = E, CC2 = B

Special Abbreviations
With yarn in front (wyif): Hold yarn to front of piece when slipping st.

With yarn in back (wyib): Hold yarn to back of piece when slipping st.

Pattern Stitches
Seed st (odd number of sts)
Row 1: K1, *p1, k1; rep from * to end.
Rep Row 1 for pat.

Block #11 (multiple of 3 sts)
Row 1 (RS): With MC, k33.
Rows 2–4: With MC, p33.
Row 5: With CC1, k1, [sl 1 wyif, k1] 16 times.
Row 6: With CC1, p33.
Row 7: With MC, k1, [sl 1 wyib, k1] 16 times.
Row 8: With MC, p33.
Row 9: With CC2, k1, [sl 1 wyif, k1] 16 times.
Row 10: With CC2, p33.
Row 11: With CC1, k1, [sl 1 wyib, k1] 16 times.
Row 12: With CC1, p33.
Row 13: With MC, k1, [sl 1 wyif, k1] 16 times.
Row 14: With MC, p33.
Row 15: With CC2, k1, [sl 1 wyib, k1] 16 times.
Row 16: With CC2, p33.
Rows 17–19: With MC, k33.
Row 20: With MC, p33.
Rep Rows 1–20 for pat.

Pattern Note
Do not cut yarns between stripes; carry colors not in use loosely up side, ready for next stripe.

Block
With A, cast on 41 sts.

Work 5 rows in Seed st.

Set-up row (RS): Work 4 sts in Seed st, work Row 1 of Block #11 pat, work 4 sts in established Seed st.

Maintaining 4 sts in Seed st each side, complete 3 reps of 20-row Block #11 pat.

With A, work 4 rows in Seed st.

Bind off all sts in pat.

Finishing
Weave in all ends.

Block to 8 inches square. ●

STITCH KEY
□ MC
■ CC1
▨ CC2
□ K on RS, p on WS
– P on RS, k on WS
⌄ Sl 1 with yarn in back
⌄ Sl 1 with yarn in front

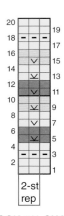

BLOCK #11 CHART

Baby Washcloths & Afghan Squares

General Information

Abbreviations & Symbols

[ ] work instructions within brackets as many times as directed

( ) work instructions within parentheses in the place directed

** repeat instructions following the asterisks as directed

* repeat instructions following the single asterisk as directed

" inch(es)

approx approximately
beg begin/begins/beginning
CC contrasting color
ch chain stitch
cm centimeter(s)
cn cable needle
dec(s) decrease/decreases/ decreasing
dpn(s) double-point needle(s)
g gram(s)
inc(s) increase/increases/ increasing

k knit
k2tog knit 2 stitches together
kfb knit in front and back
kwise knitwise
LH left hand
m meter(s)
M1 make one stitch
MC main color
mm millimeter(s)
oz ounce(s)
p purl
p2tog purl 2 stitches together
pat(s) pattern(s)
pm place marker
psso pass slipped stitch over
pwise purlwise
rem remain/remains/remaining
rep(s) repeat(s)
rev St st reverse stockinette stitch
RH right hand
rnd(s) rounds
RS right side

skp slip, knit, pass slipped stitch over—1 stitch decreased
sk2p slip 1, knit 2 together, pass slipped stitch over the knit 2 together—2 stitches decreased
sl slip
sl 1 kwise slip 1 knitwise
sl 1 pwise slip 1 purlwise
sl st slip stitch(es)
ssk slip, slip, knit these 2 stitches together—a decrease
st(s) stitch(es)
St st stockinette stitch
tbl through back loop(s)
tog together
WS wrong side
wyib with yarn in back
wyif with yarn in front
yd(s) yard(s)
yfwd yarn forward
yo (yo's) yarn over(s)

Skill Levels

BEGINNER

Beginner projects for first-time knitters using basic stitches. Minimal shaping.

EASY

Easy projects using basic stitches, repetitive stitch patterns, simple color changes and simple shaping and finishing.

INTERMEDIATE

Intermediate projects with a variety of stitches, mid-level shaping and finishing.

EXPERIENCED

Experienced projects using advanced techniques and stitches, detailed shaping and refined finishing.

Knitting Basics

Long-Tail Cast-On

Leaving an end about an inch long for each stitch to be cast on, make a slip knot on the right needle.

Place the thumb and index finger of your left hand between the yarn ends with the long yarn end over your thumb, and the strand from the skein over your index finger. Close your other fingers over the strands to hold them against your palm. Spread your thumb and index fingers apart and draw the yarn into a "V."

Place the needle in front of the strand around your thumb and bring it underneath this strand. Carry the needle over and under the strand on your index finger.

Draw through loop on thumb.

Drop the loop from your thumb and draw up the strand to form a stitch on the needle.

Repeat until you have cast on the number of stitches indicated in the pattern. Remember to count the beginning slip knot as a stitch.

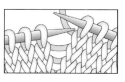

Cable Cast-On

This type of cast-on is used when adding stitches in the middle or at the end of a row.

Make a slip knot on the left needle. Knit a stitch in this knot and place it on the left needle. Insert the right needle between the last two stitches on the left needle. Knit a stitch and place it on the left needle. Repeat for each stitch needed.

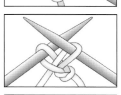

Knit (K)

Insert tip of right needle from front to back in next stitch on left needle.

Wrap yarn under and over the tip of the right needle.

Pull yarn loop through the stitch with right needle point.

Slide the stitch off the left needle. The new stitch is on the right needle.

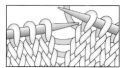

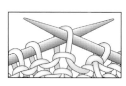

Purl (P)

With yarn in front, insert tip of right needle from back to front through next stitch on the left needle.

Wrap yarn around the right needle counterclockwise. With right needle, draw yarn back through the stitch.

Slide the stitch off the left needle.

The new stitch is on the right needle.

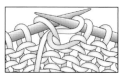

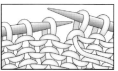

Pick Up & Knit

Step 1: With right side facing, working 1 st in from edge, insert tip of needle in space between first and second stitches.

Step 2: Wrap yarn around needle.

Step 3: Pull loop through to front.

Step 4: Repeat Steps 1–3.

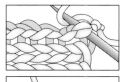

Invisible Increase (M1)
There are several ways to make or increase one stitch.

Make 1 With Left Twist (M1L)
Insert left needle from front to back under the horizontal loop between the last stitch worked and next stitch on left needle.

With right needle, knit into the back of this loop.

To make this increase on the purl side, insert left needle in same manner and purl into the back of the loop.

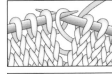

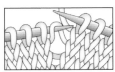

Make 1 With Right Twist (M1R)
Insert left needle from back to front under the horizontal loop between the last stitch worked and next stitch on left needle.

With right needle, knit into the front of this loop.

To make this increase on the purl side, insert left needle in same manner and purl into the front of the loop.

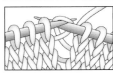

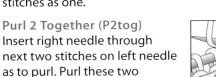

Increase (inc)

Two Stitches in One Stitch

Knit in Front & Back of Stitch (kfb)
Knit the next stitch in the usual manner, but don't remove the stitch from the left needle. Place right needle behind left needle and knit again into the back of the same stitch. Slip original stitch off left needle.

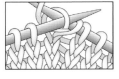

Purl in Front & Back of Stitch (pfb)
Purl the next stitch in the usual manner, but don't remove the stitch from the left needle. Place right needle behind left needle and purl again into the back of the same stitch. Slip original stitch off left needle.

Decrease (Dec)

Knit 2 Together (K2tog)
Insert right needle through next two stitches on left needle as to knit. Knit these two stitches as one.

Purl 2 Together (P2tog)
Insert right needle through next two stitches on left needle as to purl. Purl these two stitches as one.

Slip, Slip, Knit (Ssk)
Slip next two stitches, one at a time, as to knit from left needle to right needle.

Insert left needle in front of both stitches and knit them together.

Slip, Slip, Purl (Ssp)
Slip next two stitches, one at a time, as to knit from left needle to right needle. Slip these stitches back onto left needle keeping them twisted. Purl these two stitches together through back loops.

Mattress Stitch

To work this seam, thread a tapestry needle with matching yarn. Insert the needle into one corner of work from back to front, just above the cast-on stitch, leaving a 3-inch tail. Take needle to edge of other piece and bring it from back to front at the corner of this piece.

Return to the first piece and insert the needle from the right to wrong side where the thread comes out of the piece. Slip the needle upward under the horizontal thread running between the first two stitches, and bring the needle through to the right side.

Cross to the other side and repeat the same process, going down where you came out, under two threads and up.

Continue working back and forth on the two pieces in the same manner for about an inch, then gently pull on the thread pulling the two pieces together.

Complete the seam and fasten off.

Use the beginning tail to even-up the lower edge by working a figure-8 between the cast-on stitches at the corners. Insert the threaded needle from front to back under both threads of the corner cast-on stitch on the edge opposite the tail, then into the same stitch on the first edge. Pull gently until the "8" fills the gap.

Knit Side

Purl Side

Special Thanks

. . . .

Special Thanks to Tahki Stacy Charles for supplying all the wonderful yarn for this book. All of the squares were made using Tahki Yarn Cotton Classic.

TAHKI STACY CHARLES INC.
70-60 83rd St. Bldg #12
Glendale, NY 11385
(877) 412-7467
www.tahkistacycharles.com

Photo Index

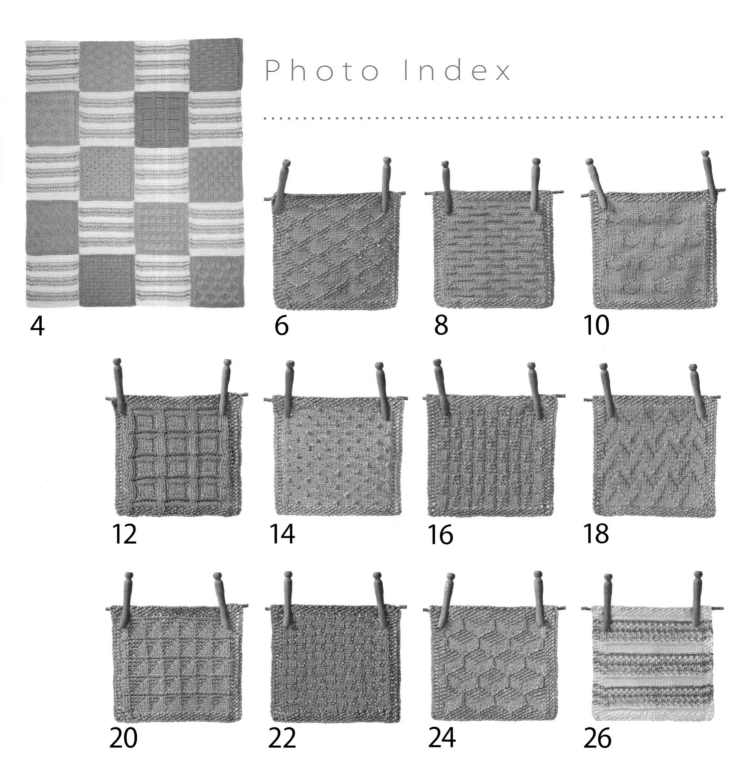

4

6

8

10

12

14

16

18

20

22

24

26

Baby Washcloths & Afghan Squares is published by Annie's, 306 East Parr Road, Berne, IN 46711. Printed in USA. Copyright © 2013 Annie's. All rights reserved. This publication may not be reproduced in part or in whole without written permission from the publisher.

Every effort has been made to ensure that the instructions in this pattern book are complete and accurate. We cannot, however, take responsibility for human error, typographical mistakes or variations in individual work. Please visit AnniesCustomerCare.com to check for pattern updates.

978-1-59635-842-3

2 3 4 5 6 7 8 9